He Carried Me

*One cowgirl's collection
of poetry, prayers, and ponies*

KATHLEEN ROSSI

petite picnic

P

PUBLISHING LLC

Petite Picnic Publishing LLC
9900 Spectrum Dr.
Austin, TX 78717

ISBN: 978-0-578-37494-9

Cover and interior design by Jess LaGreca, Mayfly Design

Library of Congress Catalog Number: 20222903264

First Printing: 2022

Printed in United States of America

To all my friends who are overcomers, two- and four-legged.
Especially my horses, "Par Four Starlight"
and "Bam Storm in the Air"

Caution: Victory ahead.
Stormy conditions favorable.

Contents

Conquest

Abide

Rise

Redeem

Ignite

Endure

Destiny

Preface

Every book has a story, regardless of the type of book it is. There has to be a reason that someone took the time to cut a bunch of words from the herd, drag them down the mountain to the wordsmith fire, and then get them all sorted out. I don't even know if people write or read poetry anymore. However, since you've set your eyes on this book, I'm assuming you might be interested in the pen it came from. And while most of the time, words speak for themselves, I'd like to offer some context by chasing a trail back that drops off into The Valley of Testimony.

Where is The Valley of Testimony? Believe it or not, you are probably familiar with the place. You may even still have the dust on your boots. It's the place you thought you might never leave and, simultaneously, the place you never thought you'd be. It's the place where conditions aren't friendly, one of its infamous landmarks being "The Loneliest Place on Earth." If you made it out of The Valley, you probably have a story that folks wouldn't believe.

Ironically, despite having the proof of tan lines and wrinkles which the heat seared into you during your trek, you somehow can't find the words to adequately express or explain how truly hot it was there. But here you are, with your worn-in sandals and blistered feet, trying to re-explain to someone the parched stupor you just lived through. They reckon you merely look like you've "been around the block a few times." All you can keep saying in your head is . . .

Trust me, you have *no* idea.

You've attempted to get the point across. Bumbling through words and mixing up sentences like switchback trails through thorny brush. Something about being stalked by a lion, not having any water, and being ravenously hungry, as well as lost. They just look at you in disbelief. Almost as if they wish you had never shared about your little trip in the first place. But then, just in case they ever end up in The Valley, you try to add on that they should be prepared to be unprepared. And that's usually when people run. You only wanted them to see the big picture: A) The Valley didn't kill you and B) How you made your way out. Instead, your postcard explanation of your trip to The Valley of Testimony is thrown out like a piece of junk mail.

I want to share the redeemed version of my story. And I think I can share enough of my testimony that presents *the feelings* the way they happened, without blatant details of how the events actually occurred. I want to show you that, despite all the pain, I experienced the wonder of being carried through that desert place. And that somehow in the mix of sweat, scars, and sagebrush, there was hope.

———•———

A few years ago, still in my twenties, I found myself ensnared in an undefinable illness, with debilitating fatigue. My condition was not anything that caffeine could perk up. (Believe me, I tried.) My energy was tanking not only from raising two children, but also my failing health. This led to me making increasingly frequent compromises for my survival. Constantly consuming convenience foods like organic frozen pizzas and keto-coffee protein drinks became the only thing that kept me loosely stitched together.

The last straw was when I packed away all our dishes and opted to use paper plates for all our precooked frozen microwave meals. As my condition gained velocity, I was like a robot with a rapidly depleting battery. My health plummeted towards the ground, mayday-style, out of my control. I couldn't push a grocery cart, couldn't walk up the stairs, couldn't load the dishwasher or clean the house.

It took everything in me down to the minerals in my bones, skin, and hair to keep our children fed and happy. I lost so much hair that it clogged the shower, which then flooded the entire bathroom and nearby closet. I lost so much sleep that I could practically spell out the word "t-i-r-e-d" with the veins showing through my translucent skin. And between breastfeeding hormones and malnutrition, I was as frail as a thread, ready to snap. This was something you heard about in old ladies, not twenty-somethings.

The change to my lifestyle was an unwelcome grinding of gears. Compromise, taking the easy way out, and depending on ready-made meals was foreign and repulsive to me. Since the age of fourteen, I'd usually balance between one full-time job to several part-time jobs. By nineteen, I was working four jobs, driving one hundred miles round-trip daily, taking care of my horses, as well as going to school. And by twenty, I had started my own business. It wasn't mathematically impossible; I did have four "free" hours a week.

Working *that* hard and *that* often was ingrained in my muscle memory. I didn't know another way to function. I'd been running that race at that pace for as long as I could remember. I had never not worked, and the feeling was helpless. So, when in my "youth" I felt increasingly like I was wearing lead boots in an environment devoid of oxygen, I began to go—and indeed I went—completely out of my mind and body.

The caffeine toxicity kicked my anxiety into overdrive. From a lack of nutrition, sleep, and mental clarity, I spiraled into a vortex of hopelessness. Daily migraines, excruciating neck and back pain, and overall mental malfunction took the helm, and it was complete hell. I tried my best to make little adjustments toward improvement, but with the dearth of energy and resources I had, nothing could save me from the never-ending, slow-motion storm.

I finally went to my chiropractor and demanded that they order me an MRI, because I was certain: I was dying. The right side of my head had now developed a sharp pulsing pain that wouldn't go away, I couldn't turn my neck, and I had a hard time being upright for very long—all newly developed symptoms on top of what was already swallowing me whole. They obliged and the MRI was ordered. Before I got up to leave, my doctor asked me to stand up, looked me firmly in the eye, and said with confident kindness: Remember who you are.

The soonest opening at the MRI facility was at 11:00 p.m. that evening. Before I changed clothes to enter my magnetic coffin, I knelt on the floor of the changing room. My pre-arthritic knees ached as I prayed, "God, just save me." When the technician motioned for me to climb aboard the death scanner, all I could think of was the worst. I was directed to lie completely flat and completely still; a mere blink could mess up the scan. It felt like I was dying, and with each loud pang and click of the machine, the weight of sin reverberated through my demeaned existence. I had the impression that this was how Jesus felt, as he couldn't escape the Cross, being pinned down and all. He was committed to the choice He had made, and there was no going back.

During this season of drudgery, I kept reading a story about a man from the Middle East sailing across the sea. He had a purpose, and a plan to get to the other side, but challenges kept rising and thrashing with the waves. Somehow, this man defied human nature: his patience was not tested, but rather he was quite at ease before he became shore-born. The motley crew of Jewish passengers aboard with him were not riding it out with such shalom. In fact, they questioned why they had naively boarded this thrill ride that might actually end up killing them.

"*She-shick*," I thought as I read.

These poor Jewish fishermen were not experienced storm-sailors; they were shallow water net watchers in for the ride of their life. Imagining the adjectives of this distinct guttural language, I could think of none more fitting than *she-shick*. And to these fishermen, it would have felt every bit like it sounded. Their voices and stomachs rose and fell with the waters: "Uh, hey . . . ! Captain!" Their captain was seemingly napping from the lulling of the waves. "Captain, we think we're gonna die!" Agitated, he woke and sternly replied, "Peace! Be still." Some scholars say that, in Hebrew, this translates to "Sit down and shut up." Everyone, including the waves, obeyed. There was an instant ceasing of chaos and a suddenly still atmosphere.

I got really familiar with this story as I read and reread it. I needed that "Peace, be still" moment in the worst way.

Once sandals hit the sand, the captain and "*she-shick*" crew coaxed their sea legs up shore. Immediately, they happened upon a guy who had gotten kicked out of an insane asylum.

This nutjob was making just as much of a fuss as the sea that had tried to upturn the boat. He wailed on and on, yelled obscenities, yanked out his disheveled hair, and cut himself with rocks found in the shadows of nearby tombstones. This dramatic scene left the sailors speechless, but then . . . in *one* word, the captain commands again, "Peace." Instantly, the person was released from his demons and returned to his right mind.

The storm was not for nothing.

At some point in my foggy health journey, I clearly heard an out-of-this-world riddle in my spirit: *Caution: Victory ahead. Stormy conditions favorable. Help is on the way.*

Somehow, I understood it. I knew I would be okay. Even as I was caught in this dreadful rip current, with the undertow blasting through my soul, I finally had a sense that maybe I wasn't going to die. The boat's stormy entrance, the peace in the middle, the powerful word that led to a person's freedom—it was my circumstance. And with every fraying fiber of my oxygen-depleted being, I believed I would have victory. I just had to make it through the *"she-shickness,"* hold on to the helm for dear life, and trust that help was on the way.

————·————

My giant "life X-ray" hung in limbo between doctors' offices for two to three weeks as I waited to receive confirmation of my worst nightmare. Surely, I had something wrong with my brain, a blockage of an artery, or some other looming lethal threat. And while I remained anchored to my weighty riddle, I still feared what my ears would hear. When I was finally called back to the doctor's office, they nonchalantly delivered the news to me as I nervously picked at the coarse stitching in my chair.

"It's just a tumor on your thyroid," they said. "Most likely it's benign, but if not, you can just get it removed. This does explain why you have been dealing with your current symptoms. Hyperthyroidism is an autoimmune disease that behaves in the exact ways you've been explaining you've felt. It was also noticed on the MRI that you have no curvature in your cervical vertebrae, which explains your headaches. Your brain has just been bouncing around on top of your spine with no shock absorption. Here is a referral number."

"Great!" I thought. "I have an old-people disease, with an old-people spine, in a young person's body! And, by the way, what even is a thyroid and why did a tumor decide to end up there!?"

Following my diagnoses, every avenue I pursued failed. Every doctor was booked, busy, or belligerent. No one had the time, skill, or capacity to help me. The wait felt weightier every day. For the next few weeks, I was living in the middle of a suddenly calm sea. Though shaken up, I felt assured that the next thing to happen would be progress. Every time I hit a wall with no answers, I kept hearing in my spirit, "Help is on the way."

Shore-ly, something was about to happen. A line in the sand was about to be drawn.

The puzzling riddle I'd heard earlier was confirmed the next morning. I was surfing the web through one squinted eye as the daily pain uploaded to my body, and I saw something that immediately froze my hand. A horse for sale with the name "Bam Storm in the Air." It was eerily similar to what I had heard about "stormy conditions" being "favorable." I clicked on the link for the stately big red filly. Of course, I wasn't going to pursue anything—my life was in limbo. But just a quick glance would satiate my curious disbelief that indeed a storm was in the air.

I innocently paddled into the horse's description. She was a long two-year-old, nearly 16 hands, gangly as could be, with a sweet expression and stamped with bloodlines to run a hole through the wind. Her shining hall-of-fame pedigree had golden filigree woven all the way back to another magnificent steed. He set otherworldly records on the track and lifted the heart of a nation: *the* Secretariat. And I'll be darn if she didn't look just like him. I thought, "Certainly I couldn't afford a horse of this caliber—ever in my life . . . Whoever gets her is one lucky . . ." I paused, perplexed:

One thousand dollars or best offer, it read. *This filly would make an excellent broodmare. Unrideable and crippled due to a possible genetic defect: osteochondrosis of the stifle.* The poor mare had a hole in the knee joint, right where the two bones meet. From the sounds of the ad, medical advice suggested the current owners not waste their time with any experimental treatment. And from the sounds of the owners, they were very willing to move this horse on to someone else's pasture. Rarely do people see value in something that is crippled.

I don't know what came over me at this point. The reality of my sickness hadn't changed, but I was sitting on my portion of peace, facing a not-so-distant shore where I had faith things would somehow change. Did I need another horse? No. Did I have the energy to ride the current ones I had? No. Did I think an unsound broodmare would be a good addition to my program? *No.*

But also, *yes.*

My flesh and faith rarely get along. I was tired of losing this ongoing battle to my condescending flesh, and somehow having faith in impossible, borderline-irresponsible things, picked me up.

We bought her on the hottest day that year, 108 degrees. Despite the stifling heat and her stifling lameness condition, she seemed ready and willing to show off. Running around on three legs and bucking with joy as the fourth one dangled in the mix. We got "Ready" from Early, Texas and hoped with all fervor that her nickname would be a prophetic marker in this desert of a summer.

———————•———————

August had barely begun when I was invited to a community-wide prayer gathering. It wasn't connected to a particular church, but rather a group of peculiar women. They felt a burden to engage the hearts of others to pray for those experiencing challenges, locally and nationally. The only person I knew was the lady who invited me, but I couldn't find her, and the room was filling up quickly. My five-year-old daughter had come along. She requested to sit up front, having spied a dance troupe fixing to perform at the start of the meeting. We crept in through the back but then somehow found two untaken seats in the front row.

The music began and the dancers twirled and stretched into the lyrics and melted into the rhythm of the song. It was a familiar tune to me. *Rise up*, the lyrics encouraged. *Rise like the day, rise unafraid, rise up.* The young ballerinas captivated all eyes and hearts as they moved in unison. We sat fixated, grateful for our unobstructed view. Their dancing was setting up the atmosphere for a miracle. Little did I know that in a few more 8-counts, the pirouettes would land, the music would finish, and the miracle that would rise up from their bow would be mine.

The speakers were ready to share what they had prepared for the event. Out of the corner of my eye, I noticed a younger gal around my age make her way up from the audience and approach the microphone with urgency in her step. Though she spoke boldly with her words, I could tell that the timing of her approach to the mic was not scripted, nor was it on the agenda. "I've heard the Lord say there is someone here He wants to heal. The imagery He is giving me is that this person has been struggling with headaches, and there is a very specific pain in the right side of this person's head. He is also giving me some very specific imagery of a boat." The room hushed. "Is that person here?" she asked.

Obviously, that person was me . . . wide-eyed and front-row-center.

The room listened for the proverbial pin to drop. They all looked like a flock of seagulls, acutely darting their heads to the right and left. In slow motion, I stood up right in front of the girl behind the mic. It was as if I had been planted right there for her to see. Our eyes met. "Me." I dryly gulped, "That person is me." I cringed as every person's focus (over two hundred eyeballs) shifted directly to us. This was the moment when the boat loses buoyancy and abruptly hits the shoreline with a scrape and a thud.

Into the mic she explained. The Lord had told her: *After tonight I would have no more headaches or neck pain. That tonight would be a line in the sand for my healing, and He wouldn't have brought it up unless He was going to do it. And whatever the boat imagery was, that He was going to calm everything about it and give me peace. He was going to give me confidence to walk out the rest of my healing journey and the courage to live and tell about it.*

She continued to say that God had showed her this picture of me in her mind: *I was climbing up this ladder, higher and higher, and I kept looking to my right, saying to God, "Let's go, God, let's do it! Wherever you want to go, I'll go!"* And her impression of God's response to me was Him saying, *"I'm going to take you to a new level with me, but I need you to stop climbing, let go of the ladder, and trust me."* She looked at me. I looked at her, and in slack-jawed assurance, I nodded.

That was me, indeed.

The rest of the night was a blur. I didn't know God still worked like that. Miraculous healings and holy, spirit-spoken words were for *other* people—*ancient* people with *brave* stories—not me. So many people came up to hug me and pray for me. All whom I didn't know from Adam, they spoke all kinds of life-giving words. They kept repeating that they could tell I was quiet and shy, but that my voice mattered. Over and over again, different women telling me the same thing. Even as the event wrapped up, I didn't experience a spark, see a bright light, or feel a jolt of relief in my body. I didn't feel physically any different. But what I *did* feel was an element of wonder that wasn't there before.

When I woke up the next morning at home, it was the oddest sensation. Almost like when you walk through a wall that was recently taken out in a construction project, or when you quickly pick up a gallon of milk expecting it to be full but it's weightless and empty. My neck and back felt loose. I could finally move my head and neck side to side equally. I have no recollection of ever being able to do this. Throughout my entire life, my whole body always felt like it was in a vice grip or being squeezed in someone's fist. That morning, however, I woke up feeling like I could easily slip out of myself. I finally was unhindered by an invisible barrier of torturous tension.

My healing continued to parallel the spoken words of faith and power from that divine evening. All my neck and back pain subsided, and the weird throbbing that was on the right side of my head disappeared. Never again, since that line in the sand, have I had another headache from hell. All the things I had been completely governed by, that made my whole life a Groundhog Day of pain, vanished. It was like they had never existed in the first place. And later that autumn, the tumor on my thyroid also dissolved and went away with absolutely no invasive medical interventions.

The instant physical healing that had taken place in my body took me months to mentally unpack.

I had immense gratitude that God saw me that night and freed me from all my pain. But I always went back to revel in the *way* I was healed. It wasn't fireworks, a boisterous casting out of demons, a finger-pointing, or fist-shaking circus of prayer. The power and presence of God was ushered in on a song. His kindness swept through the innocence of the dancers leaping in unity. His power effectively rose through a precise and direct word of knowledge. I heard heartfelt affirmations in my ears and felt my worth acknowledged in the voices and arms of strangers. It was the wonder of God that healed me.

———————

Years after stepping out of The Valley of Testimony, I stumbled upon an inconspicuous "lookout" point. Naturescapes that have a trail nestled within their midst often have a designated area where you can look out at the view, or a monument sharing a blurb of historic significance. This lookout point was different: it was named The Loneliest Place on Earth. God wasn't asking me to go back and revisit anything, but instead kindly suggesting I get some perspective. Coincidentally, God kept bringing me people who'd had strangely similar stories of their trip to "death valley."

I found out that a lot of these people, who suffered from a constant fight with inflammation and the chronic bullying of autoimmune issues like me, also suffered earlier in their life— just not from a disease. God caused me to examine my own rhythms of function, stress habits, and mental patterns that had become a part of my lifestyle. In doing so, I discovered roots of fear, trauma, and sickness, all buried in an inconspicuously dark place called childhood. The problems of my body attacking itself, the chronic pain and fatigue—these were actually *not* my fault. I had been a slave in my own body not because of a random health scare, after all, but because of redeemable human scars.

I've always enjoyed quotes such as "Don't look back; you are going *that* way" and "You aren't a tree. If you don't like where you live, move!" I proudly lived by these progressive statements, case in point having moved twenty-six times by the time I was thirty. I was happy to leave toxicity in the dust and was not the type of person to stay very long in a place of compromise. If my olfactory senses picked up the slightest hint of fermenting cow manure, I made an effort to cleanse it off my radar as soon as possible. Staying upwind was always a good place for me.

But then, one day, I read it . . . a scientific case study that summarized the same palm-sweating, stomach-dropping facts that I'd faced on the lookout point. The abstract of the article blatantly read: "*Childhood* traumatic stress increases the likelihood of hospitalization with a diagnosed autoimmune disease *decades* into adulthood" (my emphasis)*. I apprehensively thumbed through the article as it explained the measurable means between the correlation of Adverse Childhood

Experiences (ACE) to adulthood illnesses. It listed eighteen specific questions in a table that gave a score based on the prevalence of abuse, neglect, and dysfunction in the home. That hazy Valley of Testimony that I had walked through as an adult was abruptly illuminated by the truth of what had really happened when I was a kid. The breeze shifted, and I became suddenly aware that I was downwind of something that smelled very, very bad.

The study summarized that childhood stress *equals* consequences in adulthood health. There was a direct correlation between those hospitalized for twenty-one different types of diseases and those abused as children (finding relevance in their life on the ACE table). The facts were staggering—and familiar. Like the hospitalized victims, I could also empathize with the ill effects of Adverse Childhood Experiences. Of the 18 questions on the ACE table defining the types and prevalence of abuse, mental illness, and violence in the home, I could easily agree that as a child I experienced 14 out of 18. How devastating that, for some people, the level of their suffering was so high that they needed to be treated and/or hospitalized.

This leads me to wonder how many people don't speak up as children, because they too think their circumstances are "normal." Keep in mind that I did not seek help, because my pain was familiar and an expected part of daily living. However, it was a straw that had to break the camel's back. After decades of compromise and masking trauma, my body finally crashed and burned. Had God not allowed the random shooting pain in my head when I hit rock bottom, I may never have pursued an MRI to investigate the problem, nor would I have been healed from the root of what was causing me to suffer. Why was my body in such a compromised state? Simply put, look at the root of the fruit. Just because wounds are hidden, doesn't mean they are not there.

Agonizing pain and suffering is *not normal*, and agonizing pain is *not causeless*. These are two factors that I didn't quite grasp as truth, but passively let lie next to me and steal my life. Nagging mental and physical stress in adulthood can be a pest but were now an identifiable thief and killer. You can't water a plant with poison and expect it to produce fruit. The scientific research plaited together validation for me, that what I went through was not pretend just because I didn't have a voice. And just because the volume of the lies was so loud, I wasn't required to make them part of my life's song.

This book is the redeemed version of my story.

Thankfully, I learned with love and patience that nothing is broken beyond repair. During this time of healing, I gained more insight from that high and lonely lookout point. I started to hear truth and let it permeate my spirit in wonderful, creative, loving ways. Often, it would feel like a lullaby: soothing, simple, repetitive. Other times, it would ascend to the pitch of an "amp-up anthem." And sometimes it would unpack itself like a promising puzzle with a complexity you could chew on. After that healing line in the sand, I could finally hear The Love of My Life singing over me. I could hear the lyrics roll in, twirl around, and jump in time to the cadence of His heart. I was stirred to new life and perspective and I couldn't help but sing back.

The music my soul heard gave my heart uplifting verbiage, proving that, despite the storm, God was in the boat the whole time. It proved that He carried me out of The Valley of Testimony, and that He stood with me up on the lookout point. He took someone that nobody knew, stood next to, or stood up for, and personally made all the crooked things straight. I learned that victory rides in on the wings of a storm, and that God is faithful to do what He says. Help showed up for me and drew a line in the sand.

A few years after overcoming this trial, I felt that I needed to collect all the rocks from my journey through The Valley of Testimony and compile them. The truth rumbled around inside of me long enough that the edges got knocked off, and it began to turn into something sparkly. Despite the budding glimmer, I did not yet want to share the rocks from my trip with anyone. But I felt the Lord was solemnly beckoning me to do it. God asked me to pause from my many projects and be invested in finding a way to share how He carried me. This collection of writings is a reflection of how He did that.

I'm blessed to have had the opportunity to let Truth transform my life. It was sharper than any double-edged sword, penetrating deep enough to divide my soul and spirit, joints and marrow; it rightfully and lovingly judged the thoughts and attitudes of my heart. It did *not* cut me down, unlike every other word once directed at me. *Instead*, He got to the root of the problem, called evil "evil," and called me good. I am restored by God's compassion for me, and by His justice that rose on my behalf. I am redeemed by His healing, and by His truth which grows through me.

Life and death are in the power of the tongue. It is no surprise that I was revived by the Living Word, for I was literally suffocating from the lies which were trying to strangle me and take my voice. Because of God, my heart can sing a new song. I hope that if you feel stifled, invisible, or unvalued, your heart can remain open to the wonder of how the Lord can move. And even if you don't understand your circumstances, who God is, or what you are going to do, I hope these words can swirl around in your soul as an offering to stir up new life in you.

Introduction

We were not haphazardly created in the similar image of another human, but intentionally formed in the image of our Creator. As individuals, we will never—or rarely—see things the exact same way. Different seats at the table all offer different viewpoints of the focal centerpiece. We may be similar in our humanity; however, *no one* has had our walk and talk with God. We are billions of unique individuals, each with our own unique experiences, having formed a tapestry of unique personal testimonies.

Sharing ideas is hard. Sometimes we mow over manners in our attempts to pipeline a concept to someone who, in their own mind, body, and soul, is totally unique. We occasionally lose tolerance of another's learning process or personal point of view because it isn't identical to our own. The value of the message can become lost as we get tangled in a web of feelings hosted in frustration. If we remember that truth is steadfast and never-changing, but that people are individuals, then our viewpoint, mindset, and understanding can grow in revelation.

I believe our diverse perspectives were created on purpose! Why? So that God could reveal His character to us. God is living and created all living things. And despite our flawed tendencies, warped ways of thinking, and skewed views, we have an enormous capacity to receive grace and mercy. With this, we can properly align ourselves with the truth and have tolerance for the learning process. This poetic collection is a gathering of my thoughts on Who the Lord is to me, and my experiences with Him.

My surrounding environment lends me a lot of inspiration. The amount of time I spend outside with horses and livestock buddies up next to being a wife, mom, and raising my family at home. Perhaps we share similarities of a countrified "cowboy" way of life, or maybe you've never been around a pony except at a county fair. Maybe you grew up around a table bolstered by God-fearing parents, or maybe God is still a far-off "concept" to you. My walk in the woods might be different from your walk—but certainly you'd be able to relate to the way it feels to wander through the wilderness with no map or compass.

I hope you can appreciate The Map I found, The Compass I value, and how The Truth has led me. My aim is for you to see that your own wandering hasn't been for nothing, and that the Maker of your Map has had a plan for you all along. On my journey, I experienced the exhilaration of *conquest* and found value in *abiding* friends. I had to submit to the reality that I couldn't *rise* in recovery or receive *redemption* for lost things without a savior. And through this I discovered a new passion was *ignited* in me, which gave me strength to *endure* until reaching my *destination*.

The nature of a poetry collection is different from your typical read-through book. Poetry reveals a glimpse of something caught with a certain light grazing over it. It causes us to chew the cud, over and over again, of what it is saying. Poetry is about the experience: it causes us to take our time, slow down, and savor the rhyme, rhythm, and canter of the message. Read it bit by bit and enjoy your time between the pages. The time spent in this process is yours to treasure.

Conquest

TREASURE HUNTERS

This is for the dirt slingers
the daydreamers
the early risers the night doesn't tire.

For those digging for a legend of gold
with a muddy shovel, calloused hands,
and no guarantee.

The ground below is wet with sweat.
For those whose perspiration means they haven't given up yet.
Their foreheads glisten as a foretelling of the glory to come.

There's no map for where you want to go.
Sometimes your sole just trips where it treads,
and *that* is where you start digging.

Rocks for your company as you hurl and hack away?
How was a splinter-giving shovel the only tool requirement?
You eagerly await the audible vibration of contact.

Now, when people ask about that treasure, you smile.
Because you can retell the *exact* coordinates that lead to it;
The truth is the treasure you seek.

Lies might fly like wildfire, but you can't tame this;
You can only dig for it. And when you find it,
and gaze into it—the gleam of the gold reflects its maker.

HORSEPOWER

With hushed pride, we can hear in our hearts—
   God beckoning us:

Do you give the horse his might?
Do you clothe his neck with a mane?
Do you make him leap like the locust?

His majestic snorting is terrifying.

He paws in the valley and exults in his strength;
he goes out to meet the weapons.
He laughs at fear and is not dismayed;
he does not turn back from the sword.
Upon him rattle the quiver, the flashing spear, and the javelin.

With fierceness and rage he swallows the ground;
he cannot stand still at the sound of the trumpet.

Do you catch the order here?

We didn't sculpt the strength or adorn the beauty.
We didn't knit the ability or put the vapor in his lungs.
We didn't give him the brain to anticipate, the brawn to
   lunge on, or train him to be brave.
We didn't build his frame to carry the tools we'd need for
   victory.

We didn't mount his ears on his head to listen for opportunity
    to charge,
nor did we design the divine reach of the cadence of his feet:
    1, 2, 3, 4 ... 1, 2, 3, 4.
We didn't make him eager to wait, with heart that's longing
    to run,
with nostrils that make men dread the pursuit.

See, we didn't make the seed.
We didn't create its potential.
The horse in all his regal stature and fierce glory
was a gift from God to us.

A mirror to remind us of God's power.
Not a place to gaze upon our own "goodness."

To us, the horse is the seed.
We put him in the dirt, let him work the ground,
water him with wisdom and watch him grow.

If we are watching,
we will see him rise with healing in his wings,
and if we are blessed,
we will feel the wind beneath him.
He will swallow up the pattern he was made to run on.

Know this, it is equal parts grit and reverence.
It is our job to steward the sweat in the dirt.
Our duty remains to be as humble as the dust we've been
    planting in.

The more often we plant, the more often we sow.

Our ultimate goal in pursuing excellence?
Listen up,
let God take the reins
and *have faith that something supernatural can happen.*

Because when two become one, the heart doubles in size
and we simply get to be—along for the ride.

WHAT IF

The good ones always cost us something.
That's what it takes to develop authenticity.

Partnership is when you pick the path that says *what if?*

What if the vet gives the worst report on the horse you
knew could make it all the way?
What if the X-ray shows nothing but a crack right up your
dreams, in black and white?
What if the price is too high and the pain is too deep?
What if the timeline of healing is illusive and doesn't meet the
deadline of reality?
What if the answer you get is "we are sorry, but we just don't
know"?

This is how champions are made:
in the dark, thick with dust, weighted with doubt.

*What if this doesn't work out? What if it's all a waste? What if
they're right?*

This is a game where the prize *isn't* promised.
The war you win, is the way you went.

Would you keep fighting for a friend you couldn't audibly
hear say: "stay faithful"?
All his heartbeat whispered was: "keep going, keep going."
But he couldn't tell you: "that's it, don't quit!"

What if you knew that someone had already looked at the
    rough, impossible, treacherous
road ahead and nodded to accept the challenge.

Their head down, shoulders pressed in, teeth grit to the
    wind, onward.
Marching toward the possibility of failure,
accepting nothing but forward in faith
and deaf to the naysayers, ears perked for a miracle.

He knew you'd sometimes side with doubt over what'd
    already been done.
He knew you'd get caught up in what you'd already been
    released from.
He knew you'd scrape and save for what had already been
    paid for.
He knew you'd defiantly skip over what made Him
    immeasurably sore.

But most of all . . .
He knew *you*.
Because He made you—in His image.
He already looked at the cross and then decided you were
    worth it!
Cold hard proof that shows excellence in partnership was
    worth dying for.
So, indeed, it might be worth rising for.

Over and over again.
As long as it takes.
You are *this close* because He already came so far.

If "the crossroads" stands for anything, it says:
This is not where your faith will fault you!
Don't you dare drop it!
Don't give up yet.

What if the only thing scarier than pursuing the impossible
was the chance that you'd miss the miracle you're already
   making?

WILD AND RECKLESS

We don't wander, we are wooed.

Pushing past the staked claims of our faith into the wilderness.
Subalpine levels of daring exploration with little oxygen and
    a vast view of what love can be.

Lost in the forest of His beauty, surrounded by nothing but
    grace as far as the eye can see.

There is no map here, except for where He calls you.
An oxymoron, since the warm hearth at basecamp is where
    your heart seems the most lost.

The breeze that lifts up your breath and makes your skin
    crawl isn't the wind at this elevation;
it's His presence
moving your flesh and mind to find that place through the
    trees, where the light shines.

That's where you know you need to go.
Inching your feet near a cliff at daybreak, inclining toward
    the face of a mountain
just to hear Him say:
Look at Mine.

And as you gaze into what He created and who He is,
squinting into the thick rays from the East, shivering from
    the spontaneous feeling that pushed you, your heart has
    never felt so free.

Now you know the Wild is where you are meant to be.

The odds of surviving out here are against you
but God is for you.

How can you love something that you are afraid of?
It is majesty and might.
Start with admiration, then it smiles back at you!

How can you trust someone whose lightning splits trees and
    rage upturns seas?
It is majesty and might.
Begin with respect, then the touch is tender.

But how can you follow something you want to hide from?
It is majesty and might.
Step into where the path leads.

COVERED IN DUST

I knew a potter who took some clay,
brought it to a heap on that sixth day.
As He drew it in close, a deep breath He blew:
With a little bit of dirt what can't man do?

Adam's spirit stirred and his soul shook
when he saw His glory with the first breath he took,
but mistakes were made, sin cast upon the soil.
Now a little bitty lie is where man would toil.

So, He rubbed some dirt on that man's eyes,
to bridge the gap of the great divide.
Just as blind can see and dead can walk,
He gave back the sight that man sought.

Back again . . . heap of ruins, a pile of ash,
fallen so low you could hear no crash.
The world was silent for three whole days
and in that tomb His body lay.

Who could think? How could He redeem
what is gone—and sight unseen?
Then He drew it in close, a deep breath He blew:
Just a little bit of dirt, what can't man do?

We can't forget and we can't undo
the ways that God's been good to me and you.
"Come follow me!" He tells all of us,
"Nice and close, get covered in dust!"

He's a real good potter, takes ash and toil,
brings it under command in mounds of soil—
We rise up from what we come back to:
With a little bit of dirt what can't He do?

WET DIRT

It is dead quiet for a moment,
just before your eardrums split wide open from the noise.

The chaos that followed you here is right around the corner.
Its hooves will come thundering into plain view in just a
    few blinks.
You squint at the impossibility.
It's bright as the sun glinting off the water.

He led me this far.
Your lungs gasp for air even though this is sea level.
Everything you need is in your pockets or your hands.
Everything but a way through something that could drown
    you, swallow you whole.

That's the question:
Do you let fear breathe hot on your heels and catch you?
Or do you let faith blind you?

You start to wade and you hear in your heart a murmur:
Start to wade and I'll make a way.

The ground is shaking now, the clock has run down.
You hear them all behind you, yelling—their calls reverberate
    off valley walls.

Answer the question now—the sand is shifting.

Right as you're about to faint, you smell it—
wet dirt.

It always comes before a new foundation.

Who knew the alley was the gateway you'd run through on
    dry ground?
You hope it holds till you're finished running.

Squinting.
Tears this time. Your ears hear the thundering drums and
    shouts of celebration.

The time has come to look over your shoulder and see:
the way He made was where you chose to wade—

on just a little bit of wet dirt.

Abide

RIDE IT LIKE . . .

Ride it like you stole it . . . ?

Please, that old adage is for people who cheat their way to
    the top.
People who take that four-hoofed, fire-breathing, spirited
    beauty for granted.

People who receive things as gifts handle with care—
they don't run like a thief who's scared.

Your horse needs someone who holds the reins like an
    expert,
not an ex-con.

Every stride, every step, every chance you get:
Hustle

because you know what it took to get this far.

Sit deep and breathe deeper
because you know in your heart where you're meant to go—

farther and *faster* than the rest of the herd.

You stole nothing.
You bought every second of thrill on that horse with blood.
Every tenth with sweat, and every hundredth with tears.

You paid the price: early mornings, late nights.
White-knuckled it through slick roads and prayed hard with
  heavy loads.
You don't forget what you invest in, and you remember
  when it pays off.

So, give that robber nothing but a head nod as you grip that
  leather.

You don't need to ride it like you stole it!
You are sitting on something they could *never* steal and could
  never afford.

You ride it like you earned it—
you run to win.

DEAR FELLOW BARREL RACER

Dear Fellow Barrel Racer,

Who do you think you are? Dreaming above what you are
  capable of?

Yes, you!

With your rusty old bumper pull, your 5D-caliber horse, and
  your three part-time jobs . . .
You think you could visualize yourself running down that
  Thomas and Mack Alley?
The one where champions grace thousands of fans with
  their face?
The arena where tears of victory are shed,
next to the parking lot where million-dollar rigs are wedged?
You think the announcer would ever holler your name into
  the hall of fame?

You know . . .
Your horse is too slow, your funds are too low,
your truck is too old, your dreams are too bold,
your arena is too muddy, and competition glares smugly,
your family is too tired, your time is down to the wire,
Your work schedule is too rigid, your heart is too lifted.

Who would ever think YOU could be capable of reaching
  dreams with a situation like yours?

Wait ... I think we know a few people:

Scamper was from a feedlot. Fallon Taylor broke her neck.
   Sherry Cervi lost her husband. Taylor Jacob lost her
   home. Vickie Carter was a sixty-year-old rookie.

And you are probably among them because you've lost your
   mind.
Thinking that you can't.

Because these women, they lost it all too.
But they turned their *can'ts* into *cans*, and dreams into plans.
They turned regrettable situations into remarkable recovery.
They turned down barrels into darn buckles. They turned
   failure into freedom.

So, who do you think you are?
Dreaming too big, with eyes too wide and a mind too
   imaginative ... A champion?
Only if you want to be.
That's all it takes. To believe that you can.
After losing everything and feeling like you have nothing.
   Believing that you can.

So go ahead, friend ...
What you're working with probably isn't a whole lot.
But winners believe they can go big with what little they have,
and losers think they can't—because of how much they don't.

Get on your horse, saddle up, study up, cowgirl up; do you.
Because champions aren't born, and they aren't made by
   someone else.

They are ordinary people who decided to be brave, because
they believed in themselves.

Sincerely,
Someone who knew you could do it the whole time.

DEAR FELLOW BARREL HORSE

Dear Barrel Horse,

This is for you:

for the ones we lost too soon

for the ones we had and wanted to keep

for the ones ready to leave that we won't get back

for the ones who taught us everything we know, before we
were known

for the ones who expected nothing and gave us everything

for the ones who broke our bones but mended our hearts

for the ones who gave us balance on shifty ground

for the ones who wrote new records and changed our future

for the ones who ran so quickly that time stood still

for the ones who gave us faith when none could be found

for the ones who made us ride hard and think smarter

I see you:
in every buckle we won,
every turn we took,
every mistake we fixed.

I have courage for what's ahead, because you were behind me.
I believe I can grow up in what you planted deep down.
I know how to ride, because you gave me wings.

This is for you, for making me better.

Love,
a Barrel Racer

FIRST LOVE FRIEND

How do you say *friend*?

When we were toddlers, our first *partner*, a rocking horse,
    stick horse, Breyer horse.
He's the first thing we thought about upon waking
and the first thing we laid our hands on to go play with.
The horse as a *pard*, our first love with no end.

Pretty soon we were off on our own, adventuring together.
Maybe just the round pen, but little by little and step by step,
    our confidence grew and we sat tall
in the saddle. The horse now a support underneath us,
our *buddy*, our first love with no end.

Then we grew big enough to ride, and it got even better!
Because now he could take us places; we trusted him to do
    us no wrong.
He was everything right in our world,
our *amigo*, our first love with no end.

As time ticked on, a teenager needed a tame mane to
    whisper into.
Who would be loyal enough to listen and strong enough to
    carry the cares?
Not our classmates who'd gone astray but certainly
our best *mate*, our first love with no end.

Then, finally, we are right where we are now . . .
perhaps a few winding roads left us questioning some things
    in a heavy way.
He's the only thing we've relied on this whole time,
our *friend*, our first love with no end.

How do you say: *friend?*
                      pard?
                      amigo, buddy, mate?

To a horse, we say it like this: we say it with our hand and
    not with a fist,
we say it like this because, after all, that's where our heart is.

Jesus said, reach for Him and He'll uphold you with His
    right hand.
Jesus draws us near and calls us His friend.

And a friend in Jesus is a good place to be,
because a friend that is closer than a brother is steadfast in
    adversity . . .

There's no fear in love—there's no fear in friendship,
no fear in something that knows and embraces all the pieces
    of us.

There's no fear in someone we trust,
no fear in loyalty and closeness.

There's no fear in one who is powerful and submissive all at
once in Himself.

No matter how we say it—*friend, pard, amigo, buddy, mate*—

We can count on this:
Oh, what a friend we have in Jesus, our first love with no end.

GAS STATION RAPPER . . .
(THE HOOFBEAT REMIX)

Ride it like you stole it . . .

Hell, no—like, please!
That old adage is just for people who cheat
their way to the top, like they got no handle!
They be neck deep, feet caught in a scandal.

People who take that
four-hooved, fire-breathing,
slick-haired, diamond-tacked,
blaze-faced sorrel, they trippin'!

Beauty for granted?
More like beauty—*from* ashes.
Smile—We got 'em candid,
give me grace and gladness.

BAM, you got mail,
handle with care—
You're not a sissy thief,
you don't run all scared.

Get a grip, girl, whoa—
Hold the reins,
you're an expert,
you overcome your pain.

Up all night just
studying your reruns—
bruised shins, broken heart,
missing out on all the fun.

VHS rewind—
Get some perspective:
birds' nest, eagles' wings,
there's nothing you're lacking.

Prove it's all a gift—
Just keep pushing through.
Every stride, every step,
hustle's what you do!

You know what it took
to get this far—
Sit deep and breathe deeper
'cause you know in your heart—

where you're meant to go,
what you're meant to do
farther and *faster*
than the rest of the crew.

You heard that?
So don't cheat the process!
Clean slate, moving forward—
You know what the cross did.

Blood, sweat, tears, sadness.
Now you're free to run—
Get off where the fence is!
Dust off your jeans, pick up your glasses,

pedal down, mat it hard—
Siri, where the map is?!
Second again, but just by a tenth,
Wow! That makes the hundredth time?

It don't make no sense.
Now, ticktock, ticktock, count the years—
That makes a couple decades,
yikes, hold my beer.

Sober up, silly—You paid the price,
squinted early mornings and baggin' later nights.
White-knuckled it, tires slippin' through slick roads.
Praying hard, trailer shifting, weighted loads.

Horn, wake up!
You can-chasing chicken,
all your eggs in one basket—
Now, what were you thinking?

Get off of Pro-Com,
call up for some wisdom.
Bend your knee—Fix your eyes,
do you know where your yoke's from?

Tip your hat, give that robber
nuthin but a head nod,
grip that leather, grab your quirt,
spank your pony—Good Lord!

You don't need to ride
like your passin' though—
Smile big, shoulders back,
it's grit and gratitude.

Keep it in mind
and write it on your heart,
you're sitting on something
they could *never* afford.

Life bought by blood
and given by grace,
suck it up, Buttercup—
Run your race.

Keep your hat on tight,
your cash in your pocket,
penalty free—Just learn
what the law is.

Love God,
stay close to Him,
and look where you're going
if you wanna run to win.

Rise

ANATOMY OF A MIRACLE

New life on an ancient page,
the coffin bone sinking down.
There it stayed buried for three days;
death would make no sound.

Four feet on a trip to take
news that would bring the light.
What was once cold and dead
now steadily breathing life.

Heels compressed, a soul distressed;
what would good news mean?
If the ground can't hold a coffin,
there must be a risen King.

Like faithful dawn it rose again,
first a breakthrough, then a break-over.
Suddenly, a cadence heard again:
hoof beats, a musical chorus!

Fresh wind in a horse's mane,
his neck now stretching out.
Once suffocated, now circulates;
his gait does spring about!

Hear it, see it, now it comes!
Manifests what blind eyes saw!
Behold; His promise never fails.
All Glory sings of The Lord.

NO MATTER WHAT . . .
REMEMBER

Let us not forget, that You are kind and You are tender
and of all the ways You're strong and wise
this is what we will remember:

You cause the changes in the seasons,
make and take down kings.
Your eye isn't dull or blind to any troublesome thing.

Blessed are we to call You ours, it's in this title You are so,
a Heavenly Father who hears our cries,
then snaps the enemy's bow.

When we suffer in fear and feel near
the threatening sting of death—
You never fail in faithfulness to come rushing to our health.

Mighty Healer, it's You we seek for my friend and her family—
Oh Lord, rebuke, release, dissolve, and divorce
any assignment with any demonic entity!

You say freedom, peace, and grace
to all You call Your own.
You make every heart song new and give minds a healing tone.

We each go forward, brave and fierce
by the blood of the lamb—
He authors our testimony, wrote it down before time began.

Here in the gap, we intercede for my friend and all her needs.
With faith we say and sing and speak,
In Jesus' name, Rise! Sudden strength! No longer weak!

You hear that, devil?
That song is an order:
the Perfect One claimed her—get off her shoulder!

His righteousness sings peace:
Look at me, little girl
where humans have failed you—I say, *no more turmoil.*

The waves bow down,
the broken rise, then walk,
the blind can see, bad wounds heal, and the mute talk—

The fire burns up infirmities—to ashes, then beauty—
here's your testimony of new life redeemed.
Now all of heaven is moving.

STARRY NIGHT

Long ago—way back before we ever saw the star,
the words of John spoke diligently: *repent—renew your heart.*

And before we heard the angels sing about a spotless lamb,
there were a few men looking up for a light in Bethlehem.

There was a prophet or two or three—who kept on saying
    the same thing.
Decades separated them, but listen to these words they bring:

There'll be a man worth being broken,
fruit of glory that will come from a tree,
rooted, abiding and branching up through every life He'll weave.

And before that, hints and signs were seen along the way . . .
If you aren't sure, just look up the word *theophany.*

Even still, it goes back further, chasing a time-vine to a garden.
There was the Word, with God, prepared in case our hearts
    should harden.

To this day, there He remains, building but also ready;
just a nod from His Father, and in a blink—their presence
    heavy.

So, remember then, remember now, where Jesus was and is;
in reverence we bow our crowns and give a King our gifts.

HE CARRIED ME

The saddle was nice,
the rough-out stuck good;
it gave me some traction as I rode though the wood.
It sat me up straight, the horn saved my fall—
Still, that wasn't what carried my all.

The horse was built well
from his head to his tail;
he lent me some height and some legs for the trail.
He was steadfast and strong, sure-footed and stout—
Still, he wasn't who shouldered my doubt.

The map I held tight
whose binding was firm,
it taught me some wisdom and puzzles to learn.
It could be unrolled flat, or be read right to left—
Still, this wasn't what fixed me up best.

Saddle, horse, and map—the trail wove words,
of how an innocent man died a death undeserved.
All bound together with wood from a tree,
I rode still and silent—His grace carried me.

DEAD LAME

HE CARRIED ME

Lead
And
Move in an
Eternal
Direction

Are you lame, or are you learning?
The English word **lamed** means: unable to walk as the result
    of a limb injury.
But the name of the twelfth letter in the Hebrew aleph-bet
    is: *lamed* (la-med).
The Hebrew letter "L" may look lame—but it's anything but!
The *lamed* is the cultural and social equivalent of "a teaching
    stick."

Isn't it *true*
the word of the Lord is a lamp to our feet and light unto our
    path?
Isn't it *honorable*
to be shod with the gospel of peace?
Isn't there *justice*
in marching to save invisible victims and lost sheep?
Isn't there *purity*
in being washed innocent by blood and letting water cleanse
    our soul?
Isn't it *lovely*
to walk stride-for-stride in communion with Him?
Isn't it *commendable*
to walk out a mission with servant's feet?

We have the privilege of treading out a purpose on a road
that develops *excellence*.

We have the motives of mobilizing God's will, which lets
our hearts be filled with *praise*.

Whether you need your shepherd staff to prop yourself up
when you are feeling sore and tired,

as a weapon of defense to ward off bears and lions,

as a goad of leadership to drive livestock,

as an authoritative implement, striking a path through the
sea which points to the way things ought to be—the
Lord says this:

LEAN ON ME. You aren't lame, you are learning!

You are learning how to lead and move in a way that directs
your steps for taking ground for the kingdom—it is Our
Chief Shepherd's desire for us. Always being dedicated to
moving and manifesting in an eternal direction—it is
Our Creator's ambition for us.

So, **Lead** and **Learn. Ambitiously** seek Him. **Mobilize** and
Manifest His love amongst **Mankind.** With **Empathy**,
our hearts are positioned to seek **Eternal** results over
temporary compromises. Our **Destination** is our
Direction, and our **Direction** takes **Dedication.**

Redeem

THE ANXIETY A-B-CEASE!

A   Abide in God's love   John 15:9

B   Blessed are those who trust in the Lord   Jeremiah 17:7

C   Chosen by God because of His covenant   Psalm 89:3

D   David danced before the Lord   2 Samuel 6:21

E   Elohim said, Let there be light   Genesis 1:5

F   For freedom Christ has set us free   Galatians 5:1

G   Give thanks to the Lord, for He is good   Psalm 118:1

H   Happy, that's me!   Genesis 30:13

I   If you know better, don't sin   Hebrews 10:26

J   Jesus said, I'm the way, truth and life,   John 14:6
     no one comes to the Father without me

K   Kindness leads to repentance   Romans 2:4

L   Lord, you are great, there is none   2 Samuel 7:22
     like you

M	My plans for you are good, say Yehovah	Jeremiah 29:11
N	No weapon formed against you will prosper	Isaiah 54:17
O	Oh Lord! You made the heavens and earth, nothing is too hard for you	Jeremiah 32:17
P	Pray constantly	1 Thessalonians 5:17
Q	Quit and be quiet, know that I am God	Psalm 46:10
R	Rejoice in the rainbow, my promise to you	Genesis 9:16
S	Sheep know their shepherd's voice	John 10:4
T	The Lord is for me, I will not fear!	Psalm 118:6
U	Understanding comes from fearing the Lord	Job 28:28
V	Very precious! That's what you are to me	Isaiah 43:4
W	Worship the Lord with gladness, sing with joy!	Psalm 100
X	X-out fear and say "No" to sin	Exodus 20:20
Y	Yehovah bless you and keep you	Numbers 6:24
Z	Zion rejoices	Zechariah 9:9

IMPERISHABLE CROWN

The cost of a crown
low and bowed down, humbly outstretched to wash feet

Yet kind enough
to sit and rise up, saying, "Come, let us eat!"

The price of a prince
none like Him since, from beginning to end of all time

Yet common enough
to come wrapped in cloth, grown in wisdom and grace, our
   frontline.

The riches of a ruler
Who'd buy back our future, the true treasure beheld of our
   King

Yet patient enough
to forget sin-tainted past, proclaiming, "You're worth
   everything!"

We aren't just holy . . .

We don't just belong . . .

We're extravagantly saved, reserved, wholly TO Him!

It's mysterious and it's hopeful—

Expectant too

that somehow our morality holds eternal value!

The charge of Christ
spotless sacrifice, heaven's best took on the tarnish of earth.

We weren't enough
but met here in love; our High Priest intercedes for new
    birth.

NO OTHER GODS

I will
not forfeit
what's been given
as a gift

and I will not
bow down—
fear and shame
don't wear a crown.

WATER

Arks float,
seas can part.
When all else fails,
call out to whose you are.
He does not need to swim,
He is living water from a rock.
He calms the waves with His speech
and is not bound by where   He   walks.

TO BE CONTINUED

The bible is the only **book** you read that starts with *in the
   beginning*
and ends with *to be continued,*

a **manuscript** of an ancient genesis,
with the Author penning present revelation.

It is the only **text** that gives enough context to not leave
   you hanging
but beckons you into expectancy.

It contains **words** which direct steps of concreteness
from dispatchers we haven't met.

It holds the **letters** of steadfast roots of truth
and releases kingdom power in a tittle.

And *all* of it, unlike any other written work, is
Holy to the Lord.

Impressed on His hands—
Then inscribed on priests' heads,
now engraved upon ourselves in spirit.

Holy to the Lord.

The work of Our Creator is never done
because the Father's love can't be outrun.

So nestled in the plethora of never-ending oxymorons
is wisdom that leaves us undone:
The good old days are yet to come.

Therefore, everything we do is pointing to: *To be continued.*

Because of Jesus—our **High Priest**
we have the ability to intercede.

Because of Jesus—our **Worthy King**
we have power in prayer.

He changed things from a grave dead end,
to a glorious: ***To be continued . . .***

MIC DROP

I know your type, the devil said,
I've seen it all before …
You can't even stand up straight, or use your voice to roar!
You'll just sit here quietly believing all my lies.
I've trapped you—suffering silently,
alone from the inside.

But then I took the mic from him and said,
Devil, please scoot over,
I feel like I've got a Word: it's a message from my Father.

Thus saith the Lord,
Devil, what you've loosed—I've bound,
and what you've bound—I've loosed!
It's not the mic that should scare you—
but her sword in hot pursuit.

Your fun is over, time is up,
you've had one too many hits.
Unbeknownst to your serpent brain,
I've trained her not to miss.

Of course, I do not fight all by myself; sometimes I am still.
When He calls, I listen and respond
to the name He gave His girl.

Ignite

FIREFLIES

Plagued with issues left and right,
swarming at you with no end—

planning doesn't scratch the surface;
you're unraveling with no mend.

Picking out complaints to use
as if they were tools from a box—

plus, some varmints chewed tiny holes
in the big toe of your socks!

Puffed-up pride like an allergy,
a swelling poisonous bite from something—

probably won't get back to sleep,
twitchy from the buzzing that keeps coming.

POP.

Here's a new thought to the head,
an idea to hold onto—

if God can make a bug's butt light up,
just think what He can do with you!

CHAMPION

Would you have sung His freedom song
on His long hike to the cross?

Would you have called Him *champion*
when the world thought all was lost?

Would you have kept the faith despite
the fact that death is black as night?

Can you claim it personally, that He bled and died for me?
What an odd place to find victory, in a family tree.

Champion! the Father says unto His Son.
Champion! in frame for all to see.
Champion! the Son calls everyone.

And if we can see, say: He's the champion in me!

Knowing what my future holds:
God, Son of man, glory foretold.

This is where our worth will be posted,
broke through our sin His grace to boast in.

There where our worth was accosted,
for He gave all—yet never lost it.

So close to death yet He said, *live.*
Hell's keys jingled—we're forgiven.

Champion! the Father says unto His Son.
Champion! in frame for all to see.
Champion! the Son calls everyone.

And if we can see, say: He's the champion in me!

He could have called down a legion on His behalf,
stomped out all the threats right in their tracks,

He could have bailed when things were hard,
kept His skin perfect, unmarred of scars.

He could have kept the Father to himself,
sat in the kingdoms of their wealth.

No, no, no!

Because this is love:

If we can see, say: He's the champion in me!
If we know this, then this profess: He's the champion in me!

THE STIFF STUDENT

Learning new things is hard at first—

but he even loves you at your worst!

Even if you do it wrong....

he'll teach you how to sing his song.

Growing up is hard sometimes—

growing pains sure make you cry.

But if you bend your will,

he sure will like your smell!

NOSE, NECK, MAYBE THE FEET

True try has hands that keep playing till they get it right.

True confidence has a voice that says, *I'll try again despite* . . .

True grit has muscles that have strained through the test of time.

True wisdom has a mind that can follow a feel, and stop on a dime.

Faith first, feet second, fear doesn't have to follow.

THE HORSE, A PERFECT SERVANT

A horse is the perfect servant.
He doesn't ask *why*,
he just asks, *where?*

He doesn't care
if his rider is rich or poor,
athletic or lame.
He won't think twice if there is reward or fame.

A horse is the perfect servant.

He doesn't mind that his stately socks
will trudge through mud
or trot in burrs.

He wants only to be heard:
I'll go, I'll jump,
fly, or wait . . .
He won't think twice if there is reward or fame.

A horse is the perfect servant.

In his strength and beauty
he could change his mind
to prance highly someplace
nature-side.

But instead, he'll sweat and bleed to death,
pulling your load,
making your bread.

He doesn't puzzle the *how*,
he just listens for *who*

can be the one to befriend the truth.
If his rider is kind and knows him by name,
he won't think twice if there is reward or fame.

Because a horse is the perfect servant.

Endure

THE SCENIC ROUTE

Are we there yet? What about now?
No one takes the scenic route unless they're bored with no
    place to be.

You've done all you can, packed, pre-entered and planned,
then suddenly, your horse takes the scenic route to healing.

Don't panic—

whatever you do!

but don't compromise either . . .

because the enemy thrives off anxiety.

And horses can sense fear.

The *worst* thing you

can do is

get in a

bind.

You are experienced;
you know that the horse is prepared for the day of battle
but victory belongs to God.

You are savvy;
you know that a man's heart plans his way,
but the LORD directs his steps.

Even if you are blindsided by injury—*focus on the test.*

You are mature;
you know that fine wine takes time, and before that, it takes
    pruning.
And after all that waiting, you are going to sip it anyway—
You are *not* going to gulp something that you painstakingly
    grew.
Sober up, buttercup, the devil loves a dizzy fool.
You are smart;
slow down. Remember where your roots are—
you can't crumble or dry up in dismay.
The Lord will rain down His mercy, provision, and presence,
    anew!
He remembers where He planted you!

Don't just stand there!

Girl, kneel or something!

Don't panic, *whatever* you do.

And don't you dare waver either.

The Lord lavishes you in love

and a miracle might appear.

The best thing

you can do is

abide.

You serve a *just* God;
you are *not* a slave to your circumstance.

Maybe you didn't vote for the scenic route,
but isn't it about the journey anyway?

Maybe you to will learn more about each other on this
    long-awaited
traveling affair.

RUN TO WIN

I am strong since You said, *rise.*
You, Lord, have made all wrong things right.
You spread your wings over my life.

I'm going to trust again, because of where we've been.

Here we lay our burdens down,
heavy things abandon now,
weights and baggage left on the ground.

I'm going to trust again; I can feel You grin.

I ride strong, and my hands are light.
My horse is fast, Oh! he can fly.
Just look at the length of his stride ...

I'm going to trust again, because of where we've been.

I am strong since He said, *rise.*
My horse stands firm, he is ready to fly,
he tucks his legs, leaps to the sky ...

I'm going to trust in Him, we're going to run to win!

THE LORD IS MY SHEPHERD

The Lord is my shepherd
I walk the line, I walk the line
sheep behind me and to my side

I shall not want
He leads, He leads
a herd gathered, His precious sheep

He makes me lie down
all submit, all submit
we bow our knees and bend our heads

Green pastures, fount
we eat, we eat
a herd sustained, His precious sheep

He leads me now
we drink, we drink
notice nearby His sandaled feet

He restores my soul
we rest, we rest
friends gather close, relieved of stress

Our path of righteousness
He is, He is
His white wool covers all our sins

71

Death Valley I walk
He's there, steadfast
no evil befalls me, though the devil's a pest

God's authority
so sovereign
my heart is right and His presence sure

The tables are turned
justice goes
my enemies quiver, the Lord bends His bow

My head is anointed
oil flows down
into my cup and onto the ground

Goodness and mercy
follow me, follow me
all my days finally redeemed

To the house of the Lord
I come back, I come back
Here I AM—there is nothing I lack.

MUZZLE

kind   keepsake
inquisitive   impression
steadfast   serendipity
sound   steed

FRIENDS FOREVER

Whenever I think my fruit has failed,
God reminds me through friends: I'll prevail!

All of the times I feel far off and alone,
Jesus sends those who make me feel at home.

Whether in need of a laugh or in need of some help,
He causes friends to come close as joy on a shelf.

Thanks for all you are and all you do.
Just writing this to say I thank God for you!

Destiny

SECRETARIAT

By
A
Miracle

WIND WALKER

SECRETARIAT

The pioneers of the sky
wondered if they could catch the wind,
so God built them a vessel
brave enough to catch it.

When they were scared to death
to let gravity go,
the Lord gave them a mane—
strong strands of hope to lift them higher.

Impossibility blinded them with glaring challenges
but, in a blink, they received brand-new sight
and a bird's eye view between
two pricked ears.

A humility test for the pioneers' quest was offered:
a horse's only fear is *pride*.
So long as they could feel their hearts through their hands,
the reins meant freedom, friendship, forward.

A perfect design on the loins of potential.
A map, a man, and majestic steed—
a blueprint all planned by God—

To go together—do what had never been done:
To go forward, walk on wind, and bring the light of the Son.

H-O-R-S-E

If only people knew

there is so much more hoof

than hoop.

And a tad more poop to scoop.

Whoops.

DAY SIX

His hooves were rough and choppy
but his gait was smooth as glass.
Not a thing would spook him;
in steady stride, he'd pass.

He was a friendly sucker—
kind, curious, and on the move—
A nosey muzzle wiggled over
to see what God was up to.

Round and round the table spun,
clay atop the Potter's wheel—
Water, dust, pressure, mud—
All timing, balance, and feel.

God stopped the spinning, paused the pressing,
wiped off His clay-cracked hands,
turned gently toward the horse and said,
How'd you like to dance?

The eager equine's eyes lit up;
in his spirit something grew—
God smiled with a tender touch, said,
I'm making man for you!

TIMER LINE

Say you
practice your
whole life
for something
that won't
c o u n t?

Would it
still matter?

Afterword

Now, maybe you can hear the whisper of the One who spoke life, waiting on the edge of His throne to see your response. It really *was* Him the *whole* time. Singing over *you* the *whole* time. Encouraging, directing, correcting you . . . your *whole* life.

Once you've made the connection, what will you do?
Once you've tasted and seen that He is actually good . . .
Once you've started singing back to Him . . .
Once you've let Him begin training your hands after He's fixed your heart . . . What will you do?

We do have free will, you know. We can take all of the Lord's kindness, the beauty of His world, and the majesty of His creatures, and frame it. We can give our experiences a story and bend our big recoveries and adventures into our own type of glory. Most people do. His love is big enough to tolerate that for a while. He is the fullness of Truth and Grace.

But we can also exercise our free will in a different way. A way that isn't so selfish, but instead chooses to diminish ourselves and point to the only worth we have ever had, which comes from Him. His grace pours out all love, but His truth expects us to do the right thing.

Ecclesiastes 12:13 (in the Voice Translation) says the following:

And, when all is said and done, here is the last word: worship in reverence the one True God, and keep His commands, for this is *what God expects* of every person.

As your revelation of God's love for you grows— what will you do?

References

Treasure Hunters: Genesis 1:27, Romans 8:29, John 11:40

HORSEPOWER: Job 39:19, Malachi 4:2

What If: Genesis 1:10 Deuteronomy 31:7, John 11:40

Wild and Reckless: Song of Songs 2

Covered in Dust: Avot 1:4, Psalm 103:14

Wet Dirt: Exodus 14, Psalm 66:6

Ride It Like . . . : Galatians 6:9, Judges 14:14

Dear Fellow Barrel Racer: Genesis 3:1, Genesis 1:26

Dear Fellow Barrel Horse: Job 39:22

First Love Friend: Matthew 28:20, Revelation 19:11, 1 John 4:19, Revelation 2:4, Songs 2

Gas Station Rapper . . . (The Hoofbeat Remix): Proverbs 26:7, Psalm 49:4

Anatomy of a Miracle: John 20:1, 1 Samuel 16:19, Revelation 6:2, Ezekiel 37:4

No Matter What . . . Remember: Psalm 119

Starry Night: Matthew 2, Genesis 1:14, Zechariah 9:9, 1 Samuel 7:14

He Carried Me: 1 Peter 2:24, Isaiah 40:11, John 1:1

Dead Lame: Luke 7:22, Zephaniah 3:19, Isaiah 33:23, Philippians 4:8, Psalm 119:89

The Anxiety A-B-*Cease!*: 2 Timothy 3:16, Joshua 1:9

Imperishable Crown: 1 Corinthians 6:20, 7:23, 9:25, Revelation 1:6, 5:10, 1 Peter 2:9

no other gods: Isaiah 54:4, Exodus 20:3, Matthew 4:10

Water: Psalm 29, Revelation 1:5, Genesis 1:2, Genesis 7, Joshua 3

To Be Continued: 1 Peter 2:9

Mic Drop: 2 Timothy 4:17, Daniel 6:22, Revelation 12:10, Zechariah 3:2

Fireflies: Matthew 5:14, Matthew 11:30

Champion: Isaiah 53, Psalm 22, 1 Peter 2:24

The Stiff Student: Psalm 32, Psalm 119:105, Galatians 5:1, James 4:7

Nose, Neck, Maybe the Feet: Psalm 32, Psalm 119:105, Galatians 5:1, James 4:7

The Horse, A Perfect Servant: Proverbs 26:3, Isaiah1:3, Matthew 21:2, Job 39

The Scenic Route: Luke 21:9, Romans 5:4, Hebrews 10:36, Hebrews 12:1

Run to Win: 1 Corinthians 9:25, Isaiah 40:31, Hebrews 12:1

The Lord Is My Shepherd: Psalm 23

Muzzle: Job 29

Friends Forever: Proverbs 17:17, Proverbs 18:24

Secretariat: Job 39

Wind Walker: Isaiah 40:31, Job 39

H-O-R-S-E: Proverbs 14:4, Proverbs 21:31

Day Six: Genesis 1:24, Luke 13:15

Timer Line: Ecclesiastes 12:13, Matthew 20:16, Psalm 144:1

Additional References

The **preface** contains quotations, paraphrases, and summaries in reference to the following publication:

*Dube, Shanta R., DeLisa Fairweather, William S. Pearson, Vincent J. Felitti, Robert F. Anda, and Janet B. Croft. 2009. "Cumulative Childhood Stress and Autoimmune Diseases in Adults." *Psychosomatic Medicine* 71, no. 2 (Feb): 243–250. https://www.ncbi.nlm.nih.gov/pmc/articles/PMC3318917/

https://doi.org/10.1097/PSY.0b013e3181907888

The **preface** was also informed by my reading of the following:

Danese, Andrea and Stephanie J. Lewis. 2017. "Psychoneuroimmunology of Early-Life Stress: The Hidden Wounds of Childhood Trauma?" *Neuropsychopharmacology* 42 (Jan): 99–114. https://doi.org/10.1038/npp.2016.198

Felitti, Vincent J., Robert F. Anda, Dale Nordenberg, David F. Williamson, Alison M. Spitz, Valerie Edwards, Mary P. Koss, and James S. Marks. 1998. "Relationship of Childhood Abuse and Household Dysfunction to Many of the Leading Causes of Death in Adults. The Adverse Childhood Experiences

(ACE) Study." *American Journal of Preventive Medicine* 14, no. 4 (May): 245-58. doi: 10.1016/s0749-3797(98)00017-8. https://pubmed.ncbi.nlm.nih.gov/9635069/

Note: Biblical citations, verses, and references are not meant to be taken as literal translation or direct quotation. I do not have a degree in Theology, nor am I pastor. All poetic work was an artistic and creative expression of God's love by His written and Living Word. Nothing written in this book is meant to suggest that the Bible or other religious scriptures mean anything other than what they say. The scriptures that I was *inspired* by are listed clearly in "References" and taken from the English Standard Version Bible Translation . . . unless otherwise noted.

The rodeo athletes mentioned in **Dear Fellow Barrel Racer** were used as examples of those with exemplary character through exceptional challenges.

He Carried Me

COMPANION GUIDE

Get your *He Carried Me Companion Guide* online
at www.hecarriedme.com/companionguide

Download your own personal journal and
follow along with the mentorship videos.

See you there!

9 780578 374949